10-21-09

Creating Authenticity

Meaningful Questions
for Meaningful Moments

Greg Giesen

GGA, Inc. Publishers
Denver, Colorado

First Edition. Copyright © 2001 by Greg Giesen & Associates, Inc.

ISBN 0-9721114-0-9
Vol. 1

Book Design by Creative Visions
Cover Photo by Greg Giesen

WHAT PEOPLE ARE SAYING ABOUT MEANINGFUL MOMENTS

Connecting yourself to your greatness is a lifelong journey. The process begins with asking yourself the right questions. Greg's book, Creating Authenticity, helps connect you to yourself in what you value most. His book will help you savor and experience life more fully.

– Walt Kowalski
President
BreakThroughs, Inc.

This book is awesome!!! Extremely thought provoking. It enabled me to take a trip down memory lane and helped me focus on what is important to me. I thought a good idea would be to go through the book yearly and see what has stayed the same and what has changed...kind of an addition to my journal...Anyway, thanks and GREAT JOB!!!!

– Christine Steltz
Registered Nurse

I am delighted to have a copy of your new book! The idea of asking a series of questions - and such good ones - is brilliant. I imagine that many people will benefit from it.

– Pat Pendleton, M.Ed
Facilitator and Teacher
of Group Leaders

Individuals and groups must ask themselves powerful questions in order to grow and develop. Creating Authenticity is an exciting collection of questions with the power to propel people to new places.

– Douglas M. Gertner, Ph.D.
Principal, Emu Consulting

I have had a chance to experience some of the best conversations with family and friends thanks to this book. The wonderful thing is, there is no right or wrong answer.

– Barb Nation
Medical Supervisor

Hey, thanks for the book. I LOVE the questions. I've already used them and I am going to be using them for a train the trainer program in late February. Good work. I'm going to buy some for a few trainer friends.

– Jan Bouch
Management Consultant

The questions in your book are very thought provoking. I noticed a pattern in myself after the first four. Asking these questions of my kids will allow me to know them better than ever before as well.

– Jim Gadenhauf
Program Participant

This book is an asset as a training tool. Posing these questions breaks the ice within a group and sets a positive tone for give-and-take throughout the day.

– Gary Sullivan
American Water Works
Association

Greg Giesen's book, Creating Authenticity, is an amazing little gem. I have been working through it for several days now and have marveled at the thread of similarities that connect my responses. It is an excellent tool to use to become reacquainted with yourself, and to revisit your life.

– John Breed
Director of Conference
Services
YMCA of the Rockies

I just wanted to thank you for allowing me to take home a copy of Creating Authenticity when I only had five dollars on me at the time. I also wanted to let you know that your book really had an effect on me. I really want and need to figure out who I really am and what I stand for. I want to live a more genuine life. Thank you for helping me see I need to discover the real me.

– Jimmy Retana
DeVry Student Advocate

Your book seems to have covered all areas of ones life. A great deal of thought has gone into these questions—great job!

– Roger Gilbertson
Retired

This book is dedicated to my all-time favorite professor, Dr. Mac,
and to the memory of my friend and colleague, Neal Pahia.

ACKNOWLEDGEMENTS

I would like to thank the following people for their help, support and inspiration. First and foremost, I must thank my parents for being so supportive and for taking such an active interest in everything I do and have done in my life. I must also acknowledge the impact that my colleagues from the management development department at Mountain States Employers Council have had on me in multiple ways over the years. And finally, I want to thank Chip Starick, Jo Snell, Pete Grazier, Walt Kowalski, Tim Lane, and Erik Hofstetter for their inspiration and assistance in helping me complete this book.

INTRODUCTION

I created *Meaningful Questions for Meaningful Moments* for primarily two reasons. First, I wanted to provide an avenue for people to reflect upon their lives in a meaningful way. Secondly, I wanted to provide a resource that would stimulate authentic conversation between and amongst people. It is my hope that this book will accomplish both.

From an individual perspective, these questions create an opportunity to appreciate our past, to understand the present, and to identify what matters most to us for the future. It is my belief that much of who we are is made up of our experiences and the people who impacted us. By reflecting and answering the questions in this book, I have personally found myself with a self-appreciation and compassion for all that I've done, all that I've been through, and for all those people and experiences that made me who I am today. Needless to say, answering these questions was a powerful experience.

From a group perspective, I have used many of these thought-provoking questions in teambuilding, leadership retreats, and with my graduate students at the University of Denver. From a teambuilding perspective, these questions can be used as an icebreaker activity and/or as a mechanism for a group/team to better understand each other on a more in-depth level. I also use these meaningful questions in my

leadership retreats as a way to get leaders to decipher:
1) who they are, 2) who they want to become, and 3) what
matters most to them. And my graduate students particularly
enjoy using the questions to assist them in making career
decisions.

Regardless how you use this book, I hope you find these
questions helpful, both as you reflect upon your own life and
as you create opportunities for others to reflect upon theirs.
Please feel free to contact me with any questions or suggestions.

Sincerely,

Greg Giesen & Associates, Inc.
8991 South Coyote Street
Highlands Ranch, CO 80126
303-346-0183
ggiesen@juno.com • www.GregGiesenAssociates.com

WAYS TO USE THIS BOOK

Here are some ways to use this book that myself and other readers have found helpful.

By Yourself: Keep a journal and record your thoughts and feeling on particular questions as you answer them. These questions are fairly thought provoking and you may want to limit each sitting with the book to three or four questions at a time.

With Friends: Pass the book around and encourage your friends to randomly pick questions that they would like to ask the group. These questions can be particularly powerful if used in conjunction with a reflective setting, such as a campfire, or near the ocean or in the mountains.

As an Ice Breaker Activity: Put people into small groups and ask each participant to pose a question to the group for everyone to answer. Provide one book per group and have the group pass around the book for each person's turn. Since this is an ice-breaker activity, be sure to allow participants the opportunity to pass on a question.

As an Activity in a Leadership Retreat: Pre-select a few questions and divide the group up into dyads or triads and ask each group to go off and talk about the questions you selected. Give the groups a timeframe and facilitate a debrief session with the whole group upon their return. In the debrief, ask for peoples' thoughts, feelings and insights from the questions.

As Interview Questions: Meaningful Moment questions can be use to enhance your standard interviews for potential candidates. Pre-select a question or two from the book that you think would give your interview team a broader perspective of each candidate, whether it be a fun, easy question or a more serious, reflective question.

With Your Significant Other: Block out some intimate time together and take turns asking and answering random questions with each other. You'd be surprised at what you can learn about each other.

On Long Drives: Take the book with you on road trips and break the monotony of the drive by posing questions to each other.

At a Weekly Staff Meetings: Begin or end each staff meeting with a question and ask for responses. Believe it or not, something as simple as a weekly question will do wonders in bonding your staff.

If you have discovered other ways to use Meaningful Moment questions that have worked well, please let us know.

PREFACE

The following questions are meant to stimulate authentic
conversations between people. They also work well as a tool
for self-reflection. There is no right or wrong way to proceed,
so be creative and enjoy the journey.

1

TODAY

If you were told *today* that you had a month left to live, what would you want to do with the remaining time?

2

What *scares* you the most as an adult?

SCARES

What are you most *appreciative* of in your life?

3

APPRECIATIVE

4

When was the last time you cried for *joy*?
What was happening?

JOY

WANT

What do you still *want* to do in your life
that you haven't yet done?

What is one of your all-time
favorite *movies* and why?

MOVIES

SORROW

When was the last time you cried out of *sorrow?*
What was happening?

What would someone *have to do* to you
for you to end your relationship with him or her?

HAVE TO DO

9

QUALITIES

What *qualities* do your closest friends
have in common?

10

What was one of the *greatest* moments
in your life?

GREATEST

11

What was one of the biggest *obstacles* you have had to overcome in your life?

OBSTACLES

12

If you could arrange for the *epitaph* on your tombstone prior to your death, what would want it to say?

EPITAPH

13

What's one of the *wildest* things
you've done as an adult?

14

What is one of your biggest *regrets* in life?

REGRETS

ROAST

15

If a *roast* was arranged in your honor,
what three people would you pick
to roast you and why?

16

What special memories come to mind
when you think of *spring*?

SPRING

17

If you had to get a *tattoo*, what kind of tattoo would you get and where would you put it?

TATTOO

18

What's your favorite *holiday* and why?

HOLIDAY

NOT KNOW

What do most people *not know* about you?

What favorite memories come to mind
when you think of *fall*?

FALL

21

What does *spirituality* mean to you?
Do you consider yourself to be a spiritual person?

SPIRITUALITY

22

BETTER AT

What do you wish you were *better at* and why?

When was the last time you felt *powerless*?
What happened?

23

POWERLESS

24

HAPPIEST

What was one of the *happiest* moments of your life?

25

Based on your life experiences thus far,
what would be the most valuable advice
you could give to a *teenager*?

TEENAGER

26

FUNNIEST

What was one of the *funniest* things
that ever happened to you?

27

GROWING UP

What kind of a kid were you
growing up?

28

PROUD

What accomplishments in your life
are you most *proud* of and why?

Who is the *most famous person*
you ever met and how did you meet them?

FAMOUS PERSON

29

What *summertime* activities
do you enjoy the most?

30

SUMMERTIME

31

If you could *do over* something in
your life, what would it be?

DO OVER

32

FIRST DATE

What do you remember about your *first date*?

33

What is one of your favorite *winter memories*?

WINTER MEMORIES

34

MENTORS

Who do you consider to be one of your special *mentors* in the world and what impact have they have on you?

35

What are you most *passionate* about in your life?
How would someone know you were
passionate about something?

PASSIONATE

36

What was the biggest *risk*
you ever took and how did it come out?

RISK

37

How would your *best friend* describe
you to another person?

BEST FRIEND

38

What do you want to be *remembered for*
most after you die?

REMEMBERED FOR

39

TROUBLE

What is the worst *trouble* you
have ever gotten yourself in?

40

With a guarantee of *succeeding,* what would you do in
your life that you are not currently doing?

SUCCEEDING

41

When was the last time you
felt *powerful-beyond-belief*?

POWERFUL

42

FAMOUS

If you could be anyone *famous for a day*,
who would you be and how would you
spend your day of fame?

If you had the time and the opportunity
to do *volunteer* work, whom would you
most like to volunteer for and why?

43

VOLUNTEER

44

What *contributions* do you bring to this world?

CONTRIBUTION

What's been the most significant *feedback*
you've ever received?

FEEDBACK

45

46

LIKE TO CHANGE

What, in your life, would you
like to change a year from now?

47

What's your contribution to your *successful relationships*? Be specific.

RELATIONSHIPS

48

What would be the *most meaningful* thing that someone could do for you?

MEANINGFUL

What kind of things do you *complain* about most?

49

COMPLAIN

As a child, what did you want to be
when you grew up and why?

50

CHILD

51

MUSICIAN

If you could become a
successful *musician* with the snap of a finger,
who would you become and why?

52

What is one of your most meaningful
possessions and why?

POSSESSIONS

53

What is one of your greatest *accomplishments*?

ACCOMPLISHMENTS

54

SCARIEST

What was one of the *scariest* moments of your life?

55

What *trait(s)* do you most like about yourself?

TRAITS

56

What is one of the most
meaningful *compliments* you've ever received?

COMPLIMENTS

57

What was one of the *toughest* lessons
you've ever learned?

TOUGHEST

58

What *physical feature* do people
compliment you about the most?

PHYSICAL FEATURE

What do you find *attractive* in other people?

59 **ATTRACTIVE**

60 **CHUCKLE**

What past memories still makes you *chuckle* when thinking about them?

61

What is the most meaningful gift *you've ever received*?

RECEIVED

62

GIVEN

What is the most meaningful gift
that *you've ever given*?

63

When is the last time you felt *most alive*?
What happened?

ALIVE

64

What is the *best advice* you have
ever received?

BEST ADVICE

65

PET PEEVES

What *pet peeves* drive you up a wall?

66

STRESS

What creates the most *stress* for you?
How would people know
when you were under stress?

If you wrote a book on your life,
what would be the *title*?

TITLE

MOST STUPID

What was one of the *most stupid* things
you've ever done?

What *prevents* you from being as effective
as you are capable of being?

Who in your life *might consider* you to be their mentor?
Why might they say that?

71

If you suddenly had an *unplanned day off*
to spend anyway you wanted,
what would you do?

DAY OFF

72

Where would you most like to *travel* to
and why?

TRAVEL

73

When was the last time you were
filled with a great sense of *pride*?
What created that pride?

PRIDE

74

OLD-TIME

What is one of your favorite *old-time* movies? Why?

75

What *leadership traits* are most important to you?
How would people know?

LEADERSHIP TRAITS

76

CLONE

If you could *clone* yourself exactly as you are today
but have the ability to change one thing,
what would you change?

77

What *song(s)* bring back memories for you?

SONGS

78

BAD HABIT

What *bad habit* would you like
to rid yourself of the most?

What *city* brings back the
most pleasant memories for you?
What specific memories come to mind?

CITY

PERFECT VACATION

Describe the *perfect vacation* for you?
Who would you be with and what would
you be doing?

If you were going to make a movie
about your life, whom would you *get to play you?*

GET TO PLAY YOU

EULOGIZE

Assuming you had the opportunity to plan your own
funeral, who would you want to *eulogize* you?

What was your favorite *birthday* memory?
What made it so special?

BIRTHDAY

What is one of the worst things someone
has *done to you*?

DONE TO YOU

Describe your favorite way to spend a rainy *Sunday*?

SUNDAY

What is one of your favorite *childhood* memories?

CHILDHOOD

Who was your all-time favorite
teacher and why?

87

TEACHER

What is one of your favorite *television shows*
(past or present)? Why?

88

TELEVISION SHOWS

If you could have someone *walk in your shoes*
for a day to truly see your life from the inside out,
who would you most want to do that and why?

WALK IN YOUR SHOES

MEAL

If you could have any *meal* served to you for a
special dinner, what would it be?

If you could *invite* three famous people
(past or present) to dinner,
who would you invite and why?

INVITE

If you could *have any job* in the world,
what job would that be and why?

ANY JOB

93

CLOSEST TO FAME

What is the *closest to fame* that you
have come?

94

If you had to select a car that complimented
your *personality* the most, what kind of car
would you select and why?

PERSONALITY

If you had the ability to go to any concert
(past or present) and sit in the *front row*,
what concert would you go to?
Who would you take with you?

FRONT ROW

PHOTOGRAPH

What *photograph* means the most to you?

97

If you could *re-live* (but not change) a past moment in your life, what moment would that be and why?

RE-LIVE

98

LAUGHED

When was the last time you *laughed* so hard that your stomach hurt? What was so funny?

99

What would a *romantic* evening look like
for you?

ROMANTIC

100

What *possession* as a child had the
most meaning for you?

POSSESSION

101

You have just commissioned a famous painter
to do a *painting* for you.
What would you have painted and why?

PAINTING

102

ADMIRE

What person in your life do you most *admire* and why?

What is one of the most *physical*
challenges that you have overcome?

PHYSICAL

What person or memory do you remember the most
from *grade school*? What about high school?

GRADE SCHOOL

105

What was one of the worst things you ever did
that you got *caught doing*?

CAUGHT DOING

106

HAVE TO WORK

What would you do if you *didn't have to work?*

107

What was one of the most *difficult* moments in your life
and how did you *get through it*?

DIFFICULT

108

What qualities do you *have in common* with the
person(s) you greatly admire the most?

HAVE IN COMMON

What has been one of your worst
job experiences and what did you learn from it?

JOB EXPERIENCES

PAST EXPERIENCE

What *past experience* did you learn
the most from in your life?

111

Which of your *hobbies* probably
tells the most about you?

HOBBIES

112

What *motivates* you most when
performing at a high level?

MOTIVATES

113

If you could give one of your *talents* to your children or others who come after you, what would you give?

TALENTS

114

Where do you go when you need to get away to be alone with your *thoughts*?

THOUGHTS

115

What advice would your best friend most *want to give you* (knowing you the way they know you)?

WANT TO GIVE YOU

116

What are three *values* that you hold dearly and why?

VALUES

Who was one of the most *difficult* people in your life?
What did you learn about yourself from them?

117

DIFFICULT

118

If you could obtain one *characteristic or quality*
from three different people,
what would those be and from whom?

CHARACTERISTIC

119

What is still *unfinished* for you in your life?

UNFINISHED

120

What *lessons* did you learn as a child that
still impacts your life today?

LESSONS

When was the *angriest* you have ever been?
What happened to get you to that point?

121

ANGRIEST

122

If all your *body parts* could talk, which body part
would have the most to say to you or about you?
What would it say?

BODY PARTS

123

What is one of the most *challenging* things you have ever done? What did you learn most about yourself through that experience?

CHALLENGING

124

LOST

If you could get back something or someone that you *lost* in the past, what or whom would you bring back?

What is one of the most *creative* things you have ever
done or been involved with?

CREATIVE

What's different when you are truly at *peace*
with yourself and when you are not?

AT PEACE

What are you really *good at doing*?

GOOD AT DOING

127

128

SIGNIFICANT-OTHER

What have you learned the most about yourself
from past/present *significant-other* relationships?

If you could *wake up tomorrow* with
one special talent that you currently don't have,
what talent would you choose and why?

129

WAKE UP TOMORROW

130

What was one of the best *decisions* you've ever made?

DECISIONS

131

Are you satisfied with your current *health*?
If not, what would you like to be different?

HEALTH

132

If you could *move* yourself, your family, your friends
and even your work to another location,
where would you move and why?

MOVE

133

How often do you *get together* with friends?
What role do these friendships play in your life?

GET TOGETHER

134

What kind of *impact* do you want
to have on your family?

IMPACT

135

PAST MISHAPS

What critical lessons have you learned
as a result of *past mishaps*?

136

If you could have more than *24-hours* in a day,
where would you spend the additional time?

24 HOURS

Who was your *hero* growing up?
What drew you to that hero?

HERO

SUCCESSFUL

How would you define a *successful life*?
How does your life compare?

When are you the happiest?

139

140

What situations *energize* you the most?

141

What is your favorite *daydream*?

DAYDREAM

142

If you live your life to the *fullest*,
what will you have accomplished?

FULLEST

Who in your life has had the greatest *influence*
on you and in what way?

143

INFLUENCE

144

What has been one of the toughest *changes*
that have impacted your life?

CHANGES

145

What was one of the most *courageous* things
you have ever done?

146

In what ways are you *misunderstood* sometimes?

147

How do you typically handle *conflict*?

CONFLICT

148

Name a *book* or author that has impacted
your life in some way?

BOOK

What would you like to *improve* about yourself?

IMPROVE

Describe a time when you felt the most
connected to a group of people?

CONNECTED

151

What was the worst vacation you've ever taken?
What made it *so bad*?

BAD

152

If you could *reverse* a decision that you made in the past,
which one would you reverse and why?

REVERSE

What is *one thing* you would still like to learn? Why?

ONE THING

153

154

LOTTERY

What would you do if you won
a 10-million dollar *lottery*?

155

How would your mom, dad or caretaker
have *described you* when you were a kid?

DESCRIBED

156

What would you like to have *more of* in your life?

MORE

157

What would you like to have *less of* in your life?

LESS

158

What would a *perfect evening* be for you?

PERFECT EVENING

159

Have you ever really *hated* anyone? Explain.

HATED

160

What would you wear if you really wanted
to *look your best*?

LOOK YOUR BEST

If you could choose the *manner* of your death,
what would it be?

161

MANNER

162

LONELY

Do you ever get *lonely*? If so, when and why?

Would you like to be famous?
What is it that would make you famous?

WHAT IS IT

FUNERAL

If you could arrange your own *funeral*,
what would it look like?

165

What *bad habits* do you have?

BAD HABITS

166

If you could change anything about the way you were *raised*, what would it be?

RAISED

167

What makes you *insecure*?

INSECURE

168

DISAPPOINTMENT

What has been your biggest *disappointment* in life?

169

What is one of the best *conversations* you've ever had?

CONVERSATIONS

170

What type of things get you *down?*

DOWN

171

If you could select the perfect *dream* to have tonight,
what would it be?

DREAM

172

If your life goes exactly the way you
would like it to go, what will you be doing
five years from now?

FIVE YEARS

173

From your past significant-other relationships, who do you still find yourself *curious about?*

CURIOUS ABOUT

174

What has been the most meaningful *award/recognition* that you have received?

RECOGNITION

What has been one of the toughest things you
had to say to someone?

175

HAD TO SAY

Is there a past/present television *character* that you
have identified with? If so, who and why?

176

CHARACTER

177

Outside of yourself, to whose life have you
made the greatest contribution?

If you received a *lifetime achievement award* and got to
thank up to three people for their contribution to your
life, who would you acknowledge and why?

178

179

What would you *like to hear* more of that
you don't hear enough?

LIKE TO HEAR

180

If you could change *one thing* about someone important
in your life, what would you change and why?

ONE THING

What was the *closest to death* (in your mind) that you have come? What thoughts and feelings passed through you at that time?

CLOSEST TO DEATH

WORST PURCHASES

What has been one of the *worst purchases* that you have ever made?
What was one of the best?

What would make someone *dislike* you?

183

DISLIKE

184

What *attracts* most people to you?

ATTRACTS

185

What has changed the most about you
in the *past 10-years*?

PAST 10-YEARS

186

What were you *afraid* of as a child?

AFRAID

Are you ever *superstitious*?
If so, when are you superstitious and what do you do?

187

SUPERSTITIOUS

188

In order to truly live the *perfect life*,
what relationships do you need to change?

PERFECT LIFE

What has been one of the most significant things
that someone has *done for you* in the past?

DONE FOR YOU

What would be a great new year's *resolution*
for you for next year
(whether or not you believe in them)?

RESOLUTION

What *don't* you want to be remembered for in your life?

191

DON'T

PAST 30 DAYS

192

What has been the most meaningful thing
that you've done in the *past 30 days*?

193

If you could give up one *routine* in your daily life without consequences, what would you give up and why?

ROUTINE

194

What is one of your favorite *traditions*?
What makes that so special?

TRADITIONS

What *mischievous* childhood experiences
do you remember most?
What happened?

MISCHIEVOUS

195

What *single word* best describes your life
(up to now)? Explain why.

196

SINGLE WORD

197

What was one of your greatest *inspirational* moments?

INSPIRATIONAL

198

If you could *own* any company/organization in the world, what company would you own and why?

OWN

What moment(s) in *history* do you remember most?
How were you impacted?

199

HISTORY

200

SUNSET

What do you tend to think about when
watching a *sunset*?

About Greg Giesen

Greg Giesen has been involved in management development and training since 1980. With a masters degree in personnel services and counseling from Miami University, Greg spent nine years counseling, training and implementing programs as the director of student activities on the campuses of Washington University and the University of Redlands Following his higher education experience, Greg joined the world headquarters' staff of *Toastmasters International*, where he managed the membership and club development department.

Greg came out to Colorado in 1990 where he joined the management development department at Mountain States Employers Council. During his tenure at MSEC, Greg designed and presented over 20 different training courses to member companies throughout the United States.

In 1998, Greg created Greg Giesen & Associates, Inc., a leadership and management development organization out of Highlands Ranch, Colorado. His company's specific focus areas include: Management Coaching, Conflict Mediation/Training, Team Building, Meeting Facilitation, True Colors Personality Workshops and Diagnostic Assessments.

Greg is also a keynote speaker and is available for speaking engagements on the following topics:

◆ *Authentic Leadership*   ◆ *Creating High Performance Teams*
◆ *Why Conflict Matters*   ◆ *The Power of Questions*
◆ *Playing With Purpose*   ◆ *ABCs of Feedback*

Greg is also the lead-facilitator for the workshop, *Leading From Within,* a highly successful three-day, two-night intensive leadership development program. In addition, he teaches graduate courses at Denver University in the areas of leadership and team development.

To contact Greg Giesen:
Address: Greg Giesen & Associates, Inc.
                 8991 South Coyote Street
                 Highlands Ranch, CO 80126
                 303-346-0183
                 ggiesen@juno.com
                 www.GregGiesenAssociates.com

LEADING FROM WITHIN

Without a doubt, the most meaningful workshop I have ever attended.
— Danny Staples
Coors Brewing Company

Leading From Within is an intensive three-day / two-night workshop designed to help participants achieve optimal performance as a leader in both their personal and professional lives. Through the use of a variety of stimulating and challenging methodologies, participants will walk away from this workshop with a renewed sense of purpose, vision and enhanced leadership capabilities.

Program Objectives:

◆ Assess leadership strengths and growth potentials
◆ Provide a framework and learning environment where true leadership development can occur
◆ Challenge unwanted patterns of the past and recreate new patterns to live and learn by
◆ Clarify and develop a personal leadership purpose, vision and strategy
◆ Create accountability and commitment around these purposes and visions

Program Highlights:

◆ Self-Empowering Tools
◆ Centering Skills
◆ Leadership Opportunities
◆ Comfort Zone Challenges
◆ Evening Fireside Chats
◆ Solo Reflection Time
◆ Action Learning Challenges
◆ Individual and Group Feedback
◆ Individual Purpose/Vision Presentations
◆ Core Values Insights
◆ Optional Follow-Up Coaching
◆ Authentic-Self Work
◆ Leadership Models
◆ True Colors Personality Assessment

For further information on *Leading From Within*, contact Greg at ggiesen@juno.com, or www.GregGiesenAssociates.com.

It opened doors in me I didn't know existed.
— Rodney Floyd
Qwest

I'd like to thank you again for the tremendous workshop. You'd be proud of the impact it has made on my life already.
— Daniel Schmidt
JD Edwards